WE PRAY

DANIEL G. OPPERWALL

Illustrated by Jelena and Marko Grbic

ANCIENT FAITH
PUBLISHING

CHESTERTON, INDIANA

Published by:
Ancient Faith Publishing
A division of Ancient Faith Ministries
PO Box 748
Chesterton, IN 46304

ISBN: 978-1-944967-20-8

Printed in Canada

for my children
—Daniel G. Opperwall

to Anastasija and Mihailo
—Jelena and Marko Grbic

WE PRAY

Every day
to Father, Son, and Holy Spirit
whatever we are doing
and wherever we may be.

WE PRAY

Before our icons

to remember all the angels,

the saints who loved the Lord,

God's own Mother, and Jesus Christ.

Their icons tell their stories

and remind us, when we see them,

that they pray together with us

as we share their love of God.

WE PRAY

With lighted incense,
making smoke like
sweetened flowers,
for its scent is a reminder
to turn our thoughts to God.

WE PRAY

With well-thumbed prayer ropes,

each knot a repetition,

so that simple words of thanks

may flow forever from our hearts.

WE PRAY

The words of saints
from our prayer books and our memories
to learn to speak to God
as did those who knew Him best.

WE PRAY
With the "Our Father,"
special words that Jesus gave us
to teach us what to ask for,
to forgive as God forgives.

OUR FATHER
WHO ART IN HEAVEN
HALLOWED BE THY NAME,
THY KINGDOM COME,
THY WILL BE DONE
ON EARTH AS IT IS IN HEAVEN.
GIVE US THIS DAY OUR DAILY BREAD
AND FORGIVE US OUR TRESPASSES
AS WE FORGIVE THOSE WHO TRESPASS
AGAINST US;
AND LEAD US NOT INTO
TEMPTATION
BUT DELIVER US FROM EVIL.

WE PRAY

The Jesus Prayer each day,

repeating and repeating,

so that words of asking mercy

may be written on our hearts.

Lord Jesus Christ, Son of

Lord Jesus Christ, Son of God, have mercy on me, a sinner!

...od, have mercy on me, a sinner!

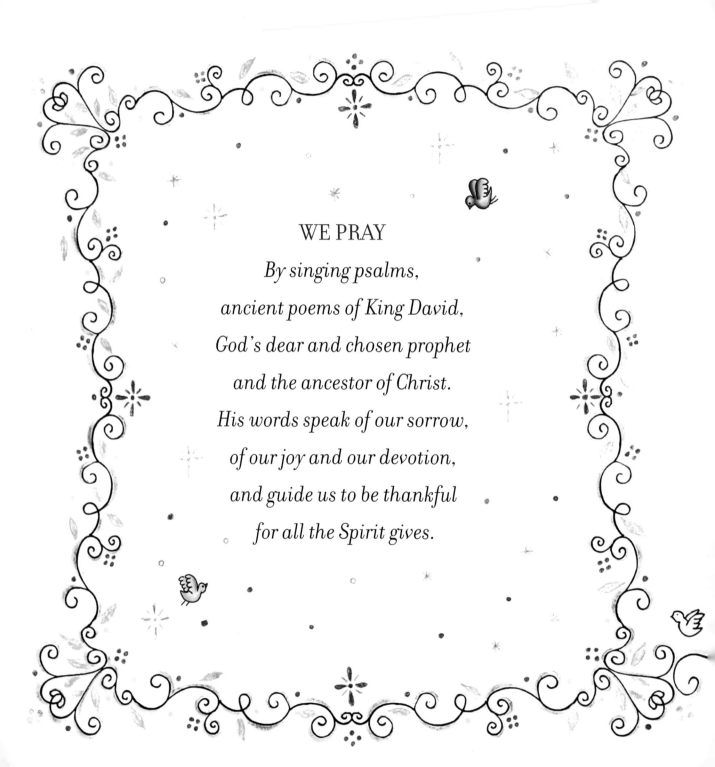

WE PRAY

By singing psalms,

ancient poems of King David,

God's dear and chosen prophet

and the ancestor of Christ.

His words speak of our sorrow,

of our joy and our devotion,

and guide us to be thankful

for all the Spirit gives.

Bless the Lord,
O my soul,
and all that is
within me
bless His holy
name...

WE PRAY

With Gospel readings,

every day another passage,

to recall the life of Jesus

and His death upon the cross.

We remember that He rose again

from death on Pascha Sunday

with a promise to return to us

and lead us to our home.

WE PRAY

*For all our families
and everyone we love,
that God's great love
would bless them
in their sadness
or their joy.*

WE PRAY

For our own bishop,

all the priests

and monks and nuns,

as they take on heavy burdens

and help guide us on our way.

The souls
of the righteous
in the hand
of the Lord

WE PRAY

For the departed,
that their souls may live forever,
and draw closer to the Savior
after death just as in life.

WE PRAY

For all the world,
every child, man, and woman,
that all may come to know God's love
and learn to seek His face.

WE PRAY

For our forgiveness

in those times when we've forgotten

to love God and each other

as He would have us do.

Our sins are separations

from the presence of the Spirit.

Through our prayers to God the Father,

Christ will wash them all away.

WE PRAY

In total silence

when our thoughts

grow still and quiet,

when grace connects us fully

to the presence of our God.

With our hearts held open to Him,

God shines His light upon us

so that we may know His Kingdom

is within us even now.

WE PRAY

At evening Vespers
for a quiet night and loving heart
that in the morning we may all
receive the Holy Mysteries.

WE PRAY

*On Sunday morning
when we gather at our parish,
to ask that God be with His Church
and present in His Gifts.*

WE PRAY

For God's real presence

in our lives at every moment,

that the Spirit guide our footsteps,

that the Son be in our hearts.

WE PRAY

for God to help us,

give us strength to do Him service,

that we shine to those around us

like lights within His eyes.

SOME PRAYERS THAT YOU CAN SAY

THE JESUS PRAYER

Lord Jesus Christ, Son of God,
have mercy on me, a sinner.

MORNING PRAYER

(A portion of the Prayer of Metropolitan Philaret)

Lord, give me the strength
to greet the coming day in peace.
Help me in all things.
Direct my will, teach me to pray,
pray in me. Amen.

THE TRISAGION

Holy God, Holy Mighty,
Holy Immortal, have mercy on us.

Holy God, Holy Mighty,
Holy Immortal, have mercy on us.

Holy God, Holy Mighty,
Holy Immortal, have mercy on us.

EVENING PRAYER

Now that the day has ended,
I thank You, Lord, and I
ask that the evening and the
night be sinless. Grant this to me,
O Savior, and save me.

PRAYER TO YOUR GUARDIAN ANGEL

O angel of God, my holy guardian, given to me from heaven, guard me
this day and save me from all evil. Instruct me in doing good deeds,
and set me on the path of salvation. AMEN.

THE AUTHOR

Daniel G. Opperwall is a husband and father of three young children. He teaches Church history and patristics at the Orthodox School of Theology at Trinity College, University of Toronto. He and his family live, read, and pray together in Hamilton, Ontario.

THE ILLUSTRATORS

Jelena and Marko Grbic, along with their two children, currently live in Belgrade, Serbia, and have recently discovered their passion for illustration. As Orthodox Christians they have enjoyed working on this beautiful book that brings an ancient Orthodox experience of prayer to children in a simple and inspiring way. The storybook reminds parents and adults alike of Christ's words, "Truly I tell you, unless you change and become like children, you will never enter the Kingdom of Heaven" (Matthew 18:3).